Harmonic Performance

Fine-Tuning Your Mind for Remarkable
Results

Mel x
Be the Creative Center of your
own life experience
Pamela x

By Best Selling Author

Pamela Mumm

Forward

The doors opened and there were 100 empty chairs spread between 14 people playing instruments. I sat next to a violinist. I thought, "What the heck is going on? I came for a leadership summit. What's this?" What followed was the most profound demonstration of effective communication I'd ever witnessed. My senses were at an all-time high. I was moved. I was invigorated.

For the next hour, Pamela and Dr. Intriligator toured me, and the other 150 participants attending the conference through various scenarios that happen every day in every organization. It was the most effective metaphor of communication I had ever experienced. The metaphor for business was undeniable for me. The musicians were the team members; the Section Leaders represented the Leadership Team and I was the maestro–the one everyone looked to for the vision, the mission and the experience that would be created within our company.

The timing of this immersive experience was critical for our company and my career. We had just come out of a financial crisis, I was dismantling the leadership team left by my predecessor, there was confusion within the organization and

I knew that we could not afford to be distracted. Our employee surveys were indicating communication problems and I needed to do something. This was the beginning of our journey to becoming a highly accountable, high-performance team.

When I was introduced to Pamela, I thought it would be the same conversation other leadership coaches had with me...here's what I can do for you, here's the astronomical rate for my services, but it's up to you, no guarantee. But, Pamela approached things differently. We talked about strengthening the business systems but that alone wouldn't be enough. There must also be intentional training to strengthen the mental game throughout the entire organization. I realized that Pamela was authoring an approach to business improvement that I hadn't seen or heard before. It was the perfect combination of Strategy and Personal Development.

This Methodology has become the cornerstone of my leadership tenants. I hope these concepts move you to think about your company, your team, yourself and how you can become the next great example of Harmonic-Performance.

Jake Schneider | Chief Vision Officer

To my parents, Donald and Carole, and my brother Scott: I love being a family with you. Thank you for loving me through every season of my life.

CONTENTS

Harmonic Performance:
Fine-Tuning Your Mind for Remarkable Results

By
Pamela Mumm

CHAPTER ONE

Introduction

Have you ever wondered why your life has unfolded the way it has? Why particular situations happened to you? Why certain people have come into your life? Why you have moved from one job to another? Why you learn some things so easily and others are a struggle?

Have you ever examined the lessons you've learned throughout your life and wondered whether those conclusions are actually serving you or getting in the way of the future you imagine for yourself? Have you ever investigated the connection between every situation, circumstance, person, experience that you've encountered and the way it has shaped your thinking? Are you ready to get curious? Are you ready to meet yourself and become an expert at being *you*?

Life will always provide the perfect curriculum so we can learn the lessons we need to learn. For me, many of those lessons emerged during the seasons of transitions: The transition from "individual performer" to leader, the transition to Executive Coach, the transition to online courses…each transition provided opportunities for intentional growth and development. My entire life had been focused on performance but these transitions would challenge me to elevate my game. You see, I had left the stage and become a high school vocal music teacher. If you've ever been in a room of adolescents, you know that you can't BS your way to success. Teenagers are kind, wonderful and ruthless. As much as I wanted to blame them, the system, the parents, the community, the world, or the universe when things didn't go well, I discovered the keys to the kingdom. I discovered that my success would be determined by my ability to deal with me.

As an Executive Coach and Professional Development Specialist, my clients say that I am the "Silent Power" behind their team, "the De-tangler" of their thoughts, the "First Officer" in their lives. I think of myself as The Mentality Maestro. I partner with people in business and together we aim high, swing for the fence, go for the gold, drop the mic, and outperform their wildest imaginations.

Let's face it, life is a series of transitions and the better we get at understanding ourselves and dealing with ourselves, the more likely we are to live the life that we imagine for ourselves.

Since thinking is shaped by our past, let me give you a peek into some of the significant moments that shaped my life.

My Map of the World

I grew up in Independence, Iowa, (no…we are not known for our potatoes…that's Idaho) a small town of just under 6,000 people. It's the county seat of Buchanan County and the "skyline," such as it is, consists of the three-block store-lined main street and the lone 6-story grist mill on the banks of the Wapsipinicon River that serves as the town's historical museum today.

Independence is in the northeastern quadrant of the state, a three-hour drive east of Des Moines, along roads lined with crops that make up America's Breadbasket. People are good, hardworking folks who believe in traditional values like going to church on Sundays, respecting your elders, keeping your yard picked up and looking a person in the eye when you talk to them. In Independence, we knew who our neighbors were, and we were always willing to pitch in when someone needed help.

My Parents

Like most kids, when I was young, my parents were my primary influencers. Sure, I had teachers, other adults, friends, and my brother, who is two years younger than me who shaped me here and there, but it was my mom and dad who were chiefly responsible for guiding me through life.

Both of my parents worked, but I wasn't a typical latch key kid. My dad worked for and eventually retired from John Deere and my mom was a cosmetologist. She owned a salon, which just happened to be in the basement of our house, so my mom was always available if we needed her. Independence is small enough to know almost everything going on and in my case, it was even easier for my mom to tap into the grapevine because of her line of work. You know how beauty salons work: she'd already heard all the juicy gossip before I even got home from school. Talk about having to be on my best behavior all the time! Whenever I slipped up, said or did something I shouldn't have like skipping band and going to Pizza Hut for lunch (because it was Senior Skip Day!) my mom would always hear about it before I could give her my version of the events. I learned the hard way that it is always better to tell on myself rather than try and change someone's mind after they'd already reached a conclusion.

Since the moment I was born, I have always been Daddy's girl. My father played a huge role in shaping me. He worked hard to be financially secure, to provide us with a nice house, put food on the table, and when it was time to go school shopping, he made sure I had my New Balance tennis shoes and Jordache jeans. Clearly, I was totally cool and trendy!

It was from him that I learned the lesson of working hard to do a job right. I still remember going out to the garage to help him with his projects. Of course, I wasn't really helping. I was too small, too young. But my dad had this wonderful way of including me, making me feel important, and even needed.

I'd work right alongside him. He'd be working on a project around the house and I'd follow him around with my little workbench. Do you remember those little toy cobbler's benches? The toy with the colored wooden pegs and the mallet. I'd diligently pound the pegs into the holes then flip the bench over and do it all over again. To this day, I still love doing projects around the house with my dad.

My mom was primarily in charge of my brother and me during the day and my God-given gifts were honed as skills because of her persistent commitment to her children. It was her hard work that paid for the dance and voice lessons. It was her long hours in the salon that earned the money to afford the cost of show choir, the travel to competitions out of town, the dresses for the performances and all those other things that go into competing at a high level. My mom is the one who would not only drive me to lessons but also sit in the car and wait for me to finish. Not a day goes by that I'm not thankful for her patience and support.

Help!

I loved singing and dancing, but academics were a different story. I remember being put in the "Turtle" reading group in third grade. I may have been young but even I knew that being a Turtle wasn't a compliment. This was unacceptable to my mother. So she hired Mrs. Greenly, a sweet and wonderful retired schoolteacher who had been getting her hair done at my mother's hair salon for years, to tutor me during the summer. While all the other kids were going to the pool, I would go to Mrs. Greenly's house to practice reading and eating cookies. I excelled at both.

I could've grown up believing that I was incapable of learning, but thanks to my mom, and people like Mrs. Greenly, I was encouraged to take on the challenge, think differently about my abilities and move beyond my limitations. Words are powerful, so why not speak something wonderful into people's lives instead of something that could potentially damage or limit them?

More Help!

Have you ever wanted something so badly and then been disappointed because your talent hasn't shown up yet? As I was going through middle school, I began to realize that my classmates were better at singing. It seemed like their vocal cords had been kissed by God while mine had been kissed by a toad. I was struggling. I couldn't match pitch and for the first time in my life I grew insecure about my voice and my ability to sing. That's when I knew that my "she's so young and cute" strategy had taken me as far as it could and I was going to need some help if I was going to make it into the auditioned groups.

Marty Dodge was my piano teacher, but we both knew that I was never going to be a great pianist. I hated practicing piano so much that I used to tape record myself practicing and then play the recording loud enough so my mom could hear it in her salon.

But singing was different. I loved singing and thankfully Marty agreed to take me on as her only voice student. I'm still amazed at the patience she displayed. Now that I've been a vocal music teacher myself, I know exactly how tedious it can be to work closely one-on-one with a student. She would hit a note on the piano and say, "Sing this back." I would listen, hear the note in my head, take a deep breath and sing, "Ah". And she'd say, "No, listen carefully. It's a little lower. I would try again this time, a little too low or a little too high. She worked with me for hours, step-by-step, note-by-note, helping me figure out how to train my ear and match pitch. It was a challenging obstacle to overcome, and Marty was always patient with me.

Marty helped me turn my love of singing into a bona fide skill. Let's face it, when you're young, you can be underwhelming and people will think you're cute. But at some point, you have to put in the time to develop the skill. While others were thinking, *Maybe you'd rather do sports* or *Maybe you'd like to try debate,* Marty is the one who saw my desire and was willing to nurture it into a skill that would be a cornerstone of my life.

Oh, in case you're wondering, when my mom finally caught me cheating on my practice time, the "Get Up 30 Minutes Early and Practice Piano from 6:00-6:30AM" season of my life began. My mom did NOT appreciate the deception!

Foreshadowing

I loved the high school experience and soaked up as many activities as I could. I was a cheerleader, sang in the choir, qualified for show choir and of course, I was in the band. We had an incredible band under the direction of Glenn Miller (not that Glenn Miller) and Lowell Ballou. I played the clarinet unless we were in marching band, where I played the cymbals.

As you already know, singing was a major part of my life and so was dancing. I started dancing when I was four years old and eventually realized I was pretty good at it. By the time I was 14, I became the youngest person selected to dance at the Miss Iowa pageant. The other dancers were all in their 20's and 30's and during commercial breaks at the event, the dancers would go up on stage and entertain the audience. My first number was doing a tap dance 16-feet in the air on a 4x8 platform…with no railing. Thank you, Rita Miller and Debbie Moser, for being wonderful teachers.

When I turned 16, my entrepreneurial spirit was kicking in and I opened a dance studio, Center Stage, with my good friend, Dawn Bearden. We taught 4-14 year olds tap, jazz and ballet, and ran the dance studio throughout the remainder of our high school years.

Life-Long Learner

After graduating from high school, I attended Wartburg College, a Lutheran school in Waverly, Iowa. I wasn't raised

Lutheran, but I was familiar with Wartburg because I had always attended their summer music camps. They had a deep and long-standing tradition of excellence in choral music and I wanted to become part of that tradition. I enrolled as a double major in music therapy and music education along with a psychology minor thrown in for good measure.

Auditions are always nerve racking. As a freshman, I was thrilled to be accepted into the Top Choir (Thank you, Marty). By my junior year I was honored to hold the title of vice president. The choir, directed by Dr. Torkelson, went on a European tour where we visited 9 countries in 30 days including East and West Germany. We went through Check Point Charlie and sold albums out of the back of our double-decker bus in exchange for vodka. I remember singing "Kumbaya" in the basement of the church with the Germans.

I was intrigued by the therapeutic quality of music and I loved psychology. It was this thought that directed me to an internship at the DePaul Psychiatric Hospital in New Orleans after the four years of course work were completed.

It was while working at DePaul that I learned to facilitate groups, working with people diagnosed with schizophrenia, multiple personality and bipolar disorders. With people who experienced sexual trauma, addiction, and co-dependency. I learned to work, stay focused and calm even in a chaotic environment surrounded by people in great need.

The internship paid a $75 stipend per week. Obviously, this wasn't enough to live on, even in a small studio apartment. So I picked up a side job. I spent my days at the psychiatric hospital as a music therapist and my nights as a ballroom dance instructor for Arthur Murray.

Bill Anderson was a seasoned professional dancer who wanted to compete in ballroom dancing and was looking for a partner. When he asked if I would consider competing with him, I was thrilled. After the studio closed for the day, we would spend hours practicing. We shared a similar work ethic and enjoyed a great chemistry between us. It was a ton of fun and we got really good. We became champions in competitions throughout the South and ranked 6th in the Arthur Murray U.S. Novice Division.

I was having way too much fun dancing to be distracted by something as minor and mundane as my internship, which happened to be the only thing standing between my Bachelor's Degree and me.

I knew I was too busy to give the internship my best effort, but I felt helpless to make the necessary changes. I was conflicted. The dance studio was paying my bills and was a lot of fun, but the internship was important, too. I needed to succeed there in order to graduate.

It was a rude awakening when, toward the end of the program, my adviser Ruth Sahuuc came to me and said, "You know, Pam, we've had a lot of interns come through this program and all of them have accomplished more than you have during your time here. In order to get credit, you'll need to stay for another three months and you'll need to show us that you have what it takes to succeed in this field."

Let me tell you, having to call my parents and tell them I was failing my internship was not a pleasant phone call to make. Humiliated, I told them that I would be staying another three months. I could feel their disappointment coming through the phone line. They hadn't paid for my education just so I could get distracted in the final chorus and not get my degree.

Throughout the remainder of the program, I was much more focused, partly because of my new-found resolve and partly because of Ruth's patient oversight and unwavering standards. I learned that once I applied myself, the work was incredibly fulfilling and I loved seeing patients get to the point where they could begin to dream a little and plan for their future.

But make no mistake. This was difficult work, work that took its toll on me. The people I worked with were incredibly troubled. While patients were going through detox, I was punched in the face, scratched and bruised. A patient pulled my sweater over my head and bit my shoulder like we were in some sort of ice hockey brawl.

I learned to keep my head on a swivel, always knowing where I was and keenly aware of who was around me. I learned how to "read a room." I could immediately identify the troublemakers, the leaders, the conflicts that existed, and the games that were being played. That skill served me well as a high school teacher, a corporate facilitator and an Executive Organizational Coach.

When my time in New Orleans had drawn to a close, I left as an RMT-BC (Registered Music Therapist, Board Certified). With my long-coming, hard-earned diploma in hand, I was ready to enter the workforce.

I got my first career job as a music therapist at the Methodist Psychiatric Pavilion in New Orleans and after five years, I realized that I was tired of dealing with the hind-end of the horse, so to speak. I was tired of working with people whose lives were already in crisis, when they were already distraught and troubled. I wanted to work with people before they were institutionalized. I wanted to help young people learn skills that would hopefully keep them out of psychiatric hospitals.

My mantra became, *I wanted to teach students about life…through music.* I wanted to help students discover the gifts God had poured into them when they were born. I wanted to guide them in how to maximize those talents so they could become positive, influential adults in their communities. I wanted to make a significant impact so my life would have meaning.

I moved back to Iowa and attended the University of Iowa where I completed my Master's Degree in one year. Making the switch to education was the right move. Being around the students was incredibly fulfilling for me. Being a part of a teaching community made me feel like I was a part of something much bigger than myself. The lessons I continued to learn were immeasurable. The folks who influenced me through those years are too many to mention here. There's nothing quite like knowing that you're in the right place at the right time, doing what you were meant to do.

But even that doesn't always last. After working in three different high schools over twenty-five years, my excitement and zeal had begun to wane. For those first seven years, I loved life and was excited to go to work every day. But now I found myself in a state of perpetual frustration. I was mad at the students, mad at the administrators, mad at the parents, and mad at the system itself. Everything and everyone was falling short of the high expectations I had set for them.

I was working 70 hours a week and I was getting little or no appreciation for all the hard work I was putting in. Couldn't they see how hard I was working? Didn't they know all the benefits the students were receiving from being in my class? Why couldn't the students work harder? Why didn't the school administration agree to fund the programs I proposed? Why are the parents nit-picking on every little thing when there are so many bigger issues that need solving? And the big one, why didn't the school promote the music programs with the energy, effort and funding that they supported the sports programs? I was mad and grouchy all the time. These questions had gotten under my skin!

I was frustrated and angry and feeling sorry for myself when my best friend, Dina Else, took me to the self-help section of Barnes and Noble. I wandered the aisles praying for a miracle. I knew I needed help and I hoped that there would be a book that had the answers I was seeking. As I searched the sea of titles, a book caught my attention. The red and black spine seemed to jump out from the others on that shelf.

The book that caught my attention that day was *The 21 Irrefutable Laws of Leadership* by John Maxwell. I devoured the information and could feel my world begin to shift. Something big was happening. We all get used to seeing the world from our own unique perspective, through our own eyes. Every event, every relationship, and every circumstance is viewed through the lens of how it affects us personally. From that perspective, things become skewed. As I read, I began to realize that the things that were going wrong in my life were simply the consequences of my current level of thinking, and the thinking informed the choices I had made.

The anger and frustration I felt weren't because of the external things like the students, the administration or the school system. The cause of all that anger and frustration was me! I was frustrated because I had become a victim in my own life. I had directed that angst outwardly thinking that something external could fix my situation instead of inwardly where it belonged.

You can't imagine the relief I felt once I realized that I was the problem AND I was the solution. As I look back over my journey, I can see the bends and the turns, the stops along the way, each point a lesson to learn, a gift to hone to make it better, sharper, stronger. Now, I leverage my musical background as a unique and different way to teach, train and coach others. Isn't that just like God? He takes our gifts in one area and reveals to us how they are leveraged in another!

This book highlights significant moments where I had the opportunity to expand my awareness and therefore expand my life. I'll share the stories, the lessons, the failures, the WINS, the tips and tricks that have helped me co-create a fulfilling and deeply satisfying life.

The mere fact that you were drawn to this book (or someone felt compelled to give you this book) tells me that you've come to a similar point of decision. You're on a journey and it's my hope that this book will provide an opportunity to observe your choices, your development and the experience you're having of your own life.

Own Your Map! Be Focused! Be Fierce!

Questions:

- What experiences stand out in your life?
- What conclusions did you draw based on those experiences?
- How have those experiences informed your map of the world?

CHAPTER TWO

Carpe Omnia

In 2003, we were on our bi-annual choir tour to New York and had scheduled several performances while we were in the City. Of course, I took care to make sure there was plenty of time for sightseeing and doing the touristy kinds of things that everyone looked forward to. I knew this would be a once-in-a-lifetime experience for many of these students, and I wanted to pack as much as possible into the trip. Times Square, Broadway Musicals, the Statue of Liberty and Central Park all made the list of sights we wanted to see.

It had only been two years since the 9/11 terrorist attacks and Ground Zero was another stop on our agenda. Visiting the site carried its own aura of curiosity and reverence. I was committed to taking the students, and I was also fully aware of the weight of that decision.

The bus pulled up to the drop-off point. The noisy, rambunctious students immediately became quiet. They knew instinctively that this wasn't the time or the place for rowdiness. This spot had become a sacred cemetery more than a tourist attraction and their reverence was required.

We were given an hour to visit St. Paul's Chapel, which sits just across the street from where the Towers fell. The church was already a famous landmark. It's the oldest surviving church building in Manhattan, and it's where George Washington knelt to pray just before walking the few blocks to the Federal Building to be sworn in as this country's very first President. Now, of course, the old chapel had become famous for something very different. Inexplicably, the building had escaped significant damage and survived the worst terrorist attack on this country's soil.

A fence, plastered with photos of people who were killed in the attack surrounded the place where the Twin Towers once stood. There were letters, flowers, candles, and miscellaneous tokens of love left by grieving family members, friends and strangers around the entire block.

The students and chaperones alike moved slowly, some in small groups, some by themselves as they followed the fence line around the block. With every step they took, they sunk deeper into their own thoughts. They didn't talk at all or if they did it was only to whisper a thought or prayer or to point out something to someone else in the group. There was no joking around, no laughing or hurriedness. This was a solemn time and easily one of the most poignant experiences of my life. But nothing like the experience I was about to have.

Thoughts Lead to Opportunities

As we were preparing for the trip, rehearsing the literature (the music we would perform), choosing the sites we'd visit and making the travel plans, I was struck with a thought: What if the choir could sing at Ground Zero? Not a performance but a mere gathering together to sing in a meaningful place. The students had been together the day the towers fell and now those same students, two years older and more mature, would travel to New York. Singing at Ground Zero just seemed…right.

As I checked my sources, it became obvious that singing at Ground Zero was highly unlikely. Understandably, public displays were being scrutinized and discouraged. Again, this was only two years after the attacks. Security was extremely high and authorities disbanded any group causing a disturbance near Ground Zero.

Once we were in New York, I discreetly asked the bus drivers and various tour guides about my thought of singing at Ground Zero. Their responses were the same. "Absolutely not!" They assumed we'd be approached by the police and told to cease, desist and disburse... I just nodded my head and said, "Alright. Never mind." But none of this took away the feeling that we were being "called" to sing. I kept all this to myself, only offering up a quick prayer, "Lord, if you want us to sing, we'll sing. But you're going to have to create just the right time for it to happen."

Confirmation

The students were wrapping up their self-guided exploration of the pictures on the fence and began making their way back toward me. They were quiet, reflective, emotional and I think seeing my familiar face was comforting, bringing them back to the safe and the familiar.

Silently, they began to congregate all around me. I remember being very still. The time slowed, and I felt we were entering into a very holy moment. From somewhere inside I heard the word, "Now" and I immediately knew that it was time to sing. There was a chance we would be asked to stop, but at that moment it didn't matter.

I looked into the eyes of the students closest to me and a student gave the beginning pitch. I raised my hand, gave a gentle gesture and almost inaudibly it began...

"Can you hear the prayer of the children..." one of my favorite songs by Kurt Bestor.

Just a small group of students humbly, earnestly, innocently sharing their hearts. As the other students heard their friends singing, they came toward us and joined, one by one, adding their energy and spirit to the moment until the entire group was there.

Crying, Jesus , help me to see the morning light of one more day...

With each line they became more emotionally connected to the moment. From overhead it must've looked like a bulls-eye, each ring of students just a little bigger than the circle in front of them, with me, standing in the center. There was no grandstanding, no instruments, no conducting...just 80 young voices processing the enormity of the experience by expressing themselves by singing a prayer.

For when darkness clears I know you're near, bringing peace again...

When the last note ended and we finished the song, there was only silence. No one moved. No one spoke. It was as if the city itself had gone silent and all you could hear were the occasional sniffles of students fighting back tears of their own. The love in that circle was palpable.

The National 9/11 Memorial and Museum hadn't been built yet. Ground Zero was still raw, and on that day, we had become a tiny pocket of life, a pocket of hope. We were surrounded by destruction and tragedy, but our gift of song, temporarily transformed that ugly site into a place of healing.

As I began to work my way out of the center of the circle, I had no idea that people walking by had stopped and were standing around listening to us. A woman, probably in her 50's approached me, hugged me and between sobs said that she had visited this spot every week to remember her husband and her daughter. Through tears, she thanked me for the beautiful reminder that one day she would find peace.

Through a small act of service, the lives of 80 high school students from Iowa were interwoven into the lives of the precious people of New York City who gathered to remember their loved ones. I was completely present to the divinity of this time and place and knew that all the hours of practice and planning, all the time spent sharpening our skills, were for this precise moment.

Presence

I believe that each and every one of us are an individuation of the universal intelligence that is God. That every situation, every circumstance and every person that intersects our path becomes our unique curriculum designed to perfectly prepare us as we grow, develop and elevate who we are becoming.

There comes a time in all our lives when we're called to step into that space that is bigger than ourselves, if we are going to truly influence our world and make a difference in the lives of others. *Carpe Omnia*, seizing everything, knowing that whatever is happening in my life is working for my good and if I haven't found the benefit, then it isn't finished.

When I was younger, I believed that God nudged other people, but not me. I thought I was left out, that God didn't talk to Presbyterians. That hearing was reserved for the non-denominational churches, the Baptists or people living in the South. Luckily, I was wrong and had to unlearn some of the thinking I had about my relationship with God.

Now, I believe God gives each of us dreams and visions for a reason. That we are all important and have a role to play in the composition of life. He gave specific dreams, talents and ideas just to you, not to your family or your church, your boss or neighbors or children. They have dreams of their own. He gave your dream to YOU. And He intends for you to seize every moment and be in tune with your life's journey. That's why it continues to burn inside you no matter how might try to ignore it.

Notice the Nudge

I've found that when I'm working with companies, groups or individuals, my focus is to help them amplify their talent and live into their BIG LIFE. Thinking back, that's exactly what happened on that sidewalk near Ground Zero surrounded by those precious students that day in New York City. The opportunity to bring healing to a painful memory was right there, all the students needed was a nudge to open their mouths...open their hearts...and begin to sing. My thoughts: "I don't want to get in trouble, I hope I don't get arrested, I hope we don't offend anyone, I hope this is OK" almost prevented a beautiful moment. It was my obedience to the nudge from the Holy Spirit whispering in my ear that gave me courage, and when the students sang, they praised God.

Many of my clients talk about the nudge that happened when they began their business, or when they were ready to launch a new line, or hire a new person, or get married or have children and the list goes on. Many talk about creating a business or a team where people can work, utilize their talents, achieve something remarkable, positively contribute to the world, and honor God.

Carpe Omnia! Be Focused! Be Fierce!

Questions:

What nudges have you felt in your life that would make life better for you and others?

What thoughts distract you when you're about to take action?

If there were no doubt, what would you do *Now*?

CHAPTER THREE

Compose Your Masterpiece

As I mentioned in the first chapter, I absolutely believe that when God puts something on your heart, it's yours. It's yours to guard, nurture, love and bring into the world. One of the presuppositions of Harmonic Performance is that everything is working for our good.

And we know that for those who love God all things work together for good, for those who are called according to his purpose. Romans 8:28 ESV

That doesn't mean life is going to unfold according to your timeline and your plan. But it does mean that every trial, tribulation, hairpin turn and sour note will provide an opportunity to learn a lesson, increase awareness and make a choice that aligns with what you desire to experience in your life.

I was always fascinated by the story of Sir Edmund Hillary. When he failed to reach the summit of Mount Everest, he was asked to attend a reception for the expedition members and speak to the audience about his experience. There was a large photograph of Mount Everest behind the podium. Sir Edmund Hillary faced the image and proclaimed, "Mount Everest, you have defeated us. But I will return. And I will defeat you. Because you cannot get any bigger, and I can."

This speaks directly to 2 Key Components of personal development: Desire and Potential. "Mount Everest cannot get any bigger, but I can." We have the possibility of growing beyond who we currently are and experiencing our life in a different way.

The Power of Desire

Desire is an idea, given to you, that's awaiting your mighty action. It generates passion, excitement, satisfaction and fulfillment. The word "desire" literally means, "to give birth to." What is it that you want to bring into the world? What do you want to sculpt? To author? To create? To compose? To build? To develop? What do you want that will enhance the world?

When people imagine and talk about their desire it changes the way they move forward. The thoughts that encourage people to remain stuck and comfortably deteriorate their way through life, lose their grip. People with desire find the energy, they allocate the resources, they develop the talent, and they reserve the time.

They say yes to the things that move them forward which automatically means saying no to things that would get in the way:

Yes, I'm open to new ideas. No, I won't resist and roadblock progress.

Yes, I'll share my expertise in a meeting. No, I won't withhold information.

Yes, I'll be accountable for my action. No, I won't blame others.

Yes, I'll decide how I spend my time. No, I won't be over-scheduled.

By focusing on our desire, our dream, our purpose, we are clear and able to make intelligent decisions. We don't say yes to avoid hurting someone's feelings or because we feel pressured. We say yes to things that help us grow, develop our skills, contribute significantly and joyfully experience this life.

Alignment with our desire brings out the best in us, increasing the experience happiness, inspiration, fulfillment, engagement, love, passion, imagination, creativity, and even possibility. When we make decisions based on desire, we are tapping into the infinite potential that lies within all of us.

Unfortunately, most people make decisions about the future they want based on the resources that are already available. When it's time to take on something new, they ask themselves, "Do I have the money? The time? The skill? The energy? The talent? The knowledge? The _____? These are all the wrong questions to ask because the answer will always be No. If we had these things, we'd already be doing and accomplishing what we want to accomplish. As we continue to hear ourselves say No, we give up on our dream. It's too much work. It will take too much time. It's too hard. We experience frustration and a feeling of being stuck. We get stuck in our relationships, stuck in our business, stuck in our lives, and as my mentor Paul Martinelli says, "Stuck Stinks!"

Luckily, there is a better question to ask. "Do I have the desire?" Obviously, the answer to this question is Yes. Can you feel the change in energy just by changing the question? This question gives our brain something wonderful to think about and since our brain is a goal-achieving machine, we get busy thinking thoughts of possibility and innovation. It allows us to tap into the improv technique of saying, Yes, And…

Yes, And here are some options we could pursue.

Yes, And here is what we can do.

Yes, And this is what I'm going to do first.

Yes, And… it allows for so much creative thinking to unleash our untapped potential.

Potential

I'm sure you've heard the quote associated with Jim Rohn that says, "You are the average of the five people you spend the most time with…" Tom Keating was the activity/athletic director and Women's Volleyball Coach when I started at Wahlert High School. When I met Tom, the women's volleyball team had won Eleven IGHSAU (Iowa Girls' High School Athletic Union) Championships. This accomplishment was unprecedented and rightfully received a lot of attention. I knew immediately that I wanted Tom Keating to be on my 5 People with whom I wanted to develop my skills, and like Mr. Keating, I wanted to become a person who could lead a nationally recognized team. Go, Eagles!

When I started at Wahlert, I decided to beef up the vocal music programs and launch a competitive show choir program. I had never launched a program before, but I knew I wanted to do something that would bring a new energy to the music program. As I was putting a plan together, I started noticing that something was off. Random thoughts were sticking in my head: What if I failed? What if we're terrible? What if my colleagues think I'm a joke? What if no one wanted to be a part of the program? I began to second guess myself and thought maybe it would be better to postpone the program until the following year.

It would have been so easy to let myself off the hook, but none of those thoughts were helping me create my desire. I wanted to create a program where students could experience being part of a nationally recognized show choir. The excitement returned. *Do I Have the Desire*? I started talking about how much fun we would have singing and dancing. Do I Have the Desire? I started recruiting students that I thought would be exceptional at helping me lay the foundation. Do I Have the Desire? I started planning the set and looking for competitions near us. Do I Have the Desire? *Yes, And* I was getting into action with steps that were aligned with the desire.

Every journey begins with a single step and ours began when 27 singers and 4 instrumentalists became the founding members of the "Impulse Show Choir." All the years of future success became possible when I started asking better questions and when 31 students bravely said *Yes, And* we're looking forward to this new adventure.

It's interesting to see how desire and potential go hand in hand when we get ready to do something new. Do we believe that we have the potential? Do we believe we can do it? Do we think we can rise to the challenge? Do we think we have the capacity to grow?

I've often heard people say, "I was too busy working IN the business rather than working ON the business to grow." I always found that confusing since growth does not happen on or in the BUSINESS. The business simply provides the opportunity, the platform where the results appear. The growth actually happens WITHIN THE PEOPLE who work within that business. Growth occurs when you are able to tap into the infinite potential that lies within the individuals who work for the organization. In other words, potential for growth happens within YOU and the results show up as an increase in life.

Live Your Desire and Develop Your Potential! Be Focused! Be Fierce!

Questions:

- What do you desire?
- What do you believe about your potential?

- What is one baby step you can take today to move toward your desire?

CHAPTER FOUR

Find Your Voice

As you have probably picked up by now, I believe that everyone has a unique contribution that they were designed to make in this world, an imprint that they will leave behind, a voice that they are meant to share.

That voice is what we use to make declarations into the world. It's the way we describe our future, what we want to experience or what we want to accomplish. It's what we want to achieve or create. It's how we utilize our unique talents and add value to the lives of others.

I was listening to a podcast about Rupal Patel. She is the Founder and CEO of VocaliD Inc, a voice company whose crowdsourced digital voices enable every voice to be heard! She talks about our voice being as unique as our fingerprints. Imagine, when we use our voice, the words we choose to describe the desires of our heart cross our lips and we begin to speak our future into existence, using our unique vocal impression.

In 2007, I began speaking my future into existence when I was introduced to the magic of Carnegie Hall.

Carnegie Hall, New York, NY

Wahlert High School was part of the 300 Singer Festival Choir performing the Mozart Requiem, K626 on the Carnegie Hall stage. The students had been preparing for months, even coming in on weekends to make sure they knew what they were doing, and by the time the performance was finished, I was in love with this perfectly designed performance hall and knew that I wanted to conduct the Wahlert Choir, by themselves, on this prestigious stage. It was then I declared that one day we would return to Carnegie Hall and perform a solo Prelude Concert.

A Prelude Concert is an opportunity for amateur choirs to perform before the scheduled headliner act and it is rare that a high school choir is awarded the honor. Of course, I had no idea how to make this dream happen, I only knew that it was exciting, out of reach and something I wanted to experience.

I started talking about returning to New York, imagining what songs we would sing. In 2009. As I was working with the men's and women's choirs, I had an inspired thought and as a bold move, I sent a letter to all the freshmen and sophomore choir parents telling them to start saving money because in 2 years we'd be singing at Carnegie.

Fast Forward...

In 2010, our day-to-day life was normal. There was literature to choose, music to learn and skills to develop. As I looked at literature for an upcoming concert, I noticed that the composer of some of the literature I wanted to program would travel and perform with choirs. That sounded fun and exciting, so I reached out to John Angotti and, through his agent, booked him for a concert later in the year. I then began the process of getting the choir ready to perform with our special guest artist.

The weekend of the concert finally arrived. We were scheduled to rehearse with Mr. Angotti and his band on Saturday afternoon for the Sunday afternoon performance. The students were all on time and patiently waiting for the band arriving from Nashville.

Students were kicking around a hacky sack outside as Mr. Angotti was getting out of the car. He offhandedly asked, "Are these the students?" I told him yes, those are some of the students. I gave a loud whistle, (which I learned at a 4th of July barn dance when I was in middle school; it has come in handy on several occasions) the kind that uses your fingers and can be heard for miles. The students all knew the whistle meant, "Come on in, it's time to get started!" As we walked into the building John saw another group of students hanging out in the lobby. He asked me, "Who are these guys?" I replied, "More students."

We continued the walk into the gym where the concert was going to be held. There were more students in there. Again he asked, "Who are they?" I laughed, "The rest of the singers!" He laughed with me as we all made our way to the performance area.

The band took a few minutes to get set up while the choir used the time to get situated on the risers. Picture this: Mr. Angotti and his band down in front. The choir, all 300 of them, are arranged on risers and platforms at different levels in a wide horseshoe around him and I'm right in the middle. We had almost no budget in those days but a group of parents had joined together to provide the funds so we could buy a beautiful black baby grand piano. It was in a place of prominence, front and center. Once we were all in our places, it was time to start the rehearsal.

After a gracious welcome and a few other introductory comments, we were ready to begin. With a booming voice, Mr. Angotti led out, "May the glory of the Lord..." And all the students boldly sang, "...Rise among us!" As soon as they completed their first phrase I saw Mr. Angotti smile. He held up his hand to stop. He looked down and said, almost to himself, "Whoa, that was awesome." Then he looked up at the choir and said, "Alright, guys. Let's do this!"

From that moment, I knew we were going to do fine, even better than fine. I knew we were in for a special experience that would move our spirits and leave a lasting impression.

Sunday arrived and I looked out at the crowd. The gym was full of parents, families, friends and community members. We had spared no amount of energy in making sure everyone in town knew about the performance. The sense of anticipation filled the gymnasium and the energy was electric.

The students rocked their performance...and so did Mr. Angotti and his band (Dion and Grady). The music was passionate as the students sang straight from their hearts. Their performance stirred emotions in the audience and I could see several people in the crowd tearing up, including me. That concert was undoubtedly one of the highlights of my teaching career.

Encore

When the concert was over and the last of the crowd had made their way out of the gym, Mr. Angotti hugged me and praised the students. They were well prepared, sounded amazing and conducted themselves in a professional manner.

I was on such a high that I immediately booked Mr. Angotti to come back and join us for the Christmas Concert. Once again, the students were awesome, the music was inspirational and energizing, the audience was dazzled. We were finding our groove and loved performing with Mr. Angotti. He was scheduled to perform at another venue in our area and after the concert, he invited us to join him at his next performance. Thanks to the generosity of the supportive parents who agreed to pay our transportation costs, we were able to say yes and performed with him at the Gallagher Bluedorn Theater on the campus of the University of Northern Iowa in Cedar Falls. It was invigorating and another tremendous opportunity!

The Call

In 2011, I called an impromptu meeting with the entire choir and any parents that wanted to attend because I had an important question to ask. I stood in front of the group and announced, "I got a phone call from Mr. Angotti. He would like us to join him for another performance ... at Carnegie Hall!" The room instantly filled with energy and excitement. "What? Yes. YES. YES! When? How long will we be there? Can we go shopping?" The questions kept coming. I just laughed. "Oh, and by the way, we will be singing the Solo Prelude Concert." I didn't know whether to dance or cry, so I did both.

I was blown away! When I sent that original letter to the parents, I hadn't even met John Angotti, I didn't know who he was. I had no idea that we would perform several times with him and I had no idea that he would be invited to perform at Carnegie Hall. I had no idea that he would invite us to join him. This is the power of using your voice to declare the desires of your heart. This step begins to act like a magnet. It has a force that moves things toward us.

I once heard a metaphor (or maybe an analogy... I always get confused: Imagine that you are in a restaurant. You call the server over and order a tender, juicy fillet, medium rare and a baked potato with butter and sour cream. The server leaves, goes to the kitchen and places the order with the chef and the chef gets busy preparing your delicious meal.

A couple minutes later, you decide that a fillet does't sound good. You'd rather have their spinach tortellini in a white sauce with some bread. You call the server over and place your new order. The server gladly takes your order back to the chef and the chef throws out the steak and starts boiling the noodles for your new meal.

After sitting for a minute, you decide that the Tortallini sounds too rich and you'd rather have a salad. You call the server over and once again change your order. The server gladly takes your order back to the chef and the chef throws out the pasta and starts chopping lettuce for your new meal.

Once again, you decide to change your order. This time you order the soup. The server goes to the kitchen and informs the chef.

In this story, the order represents desire, the server represents your subconscious mind and the chef represents Divine Intelligence or God. Every time we "place an order" our subconscious mind says OK and it gets into action helping us achieve whatever order was placed. Remember, our desires are given to us by God. When we hear the nudge, we declare our desire, knowing that God is in the kitchen working on our behalf. It may take time, but things are being prepared for us. This is when we are in alignment with our purpose. It's when our subconscious mind is focused on thoughts that are serving us and we're moving toward an experience that makes things better for the people around us.

The Program

Now it was time to prepare a program that would honor God. In addition to the 80 students, I invited the most accomplished accompanist I had the privilege of teaching during my years at Wahlert, Michael Bagby, to join us. Not only did he accompany the choir, he also premiered his original piano composition, "Bells," on the Carnegie stage.

The A cappella Choir performed an original composition by Michael of my favorite prayer. Then the rest of the Concert Choir joined them on stage. As soon as they began to sing the audience was dazzled by a tremendous wall of sound as they sang from Eugene Butler's arrangement of "Hymn of Fire." We sang about all the elements, Fire, Water, Wind and Earth and ended with, "Your God Will Come" arranged by Nick Robertson and Cliff Duren. It was GLORIOUS!

That day as I stood on the stage of Carnegie Hall conducting the students, I experienced what I would call an energetic connection. I felt as though I could reach out and touch every student even though there were several feet and rows of chairs between us. It felt as if there was no space between us. It was like we were all pure light joining together doing something we loved so much. Maureen Kuhl, a senior in the choir that year, said this before our final song:

"We are the voices in the hall, created perfectly by God to become one voice of good will. It is out of God's glorifying love that we are each a perfect combination of the elements. Each of us, inspired from within and inspired by others, are on a divine mission. And all in all, it is for the love of God that we live."

Declare It

I love this story, not only because it is a wonderful memory from my teaching days but also because it's such a great lesson about the power of declaring something, out loud, even though you have no idea how to accomplish it. It's about visioning, imagining, and dreaming.

It reminds me of working with a client, Sarah. The first day she came into my office to talk, we had just finished a dream brainstorming session with the team; we were narrowing down what she wanted to create. She began to cry and said, "I want to find my voice. I'm tired of being known as my husband's wife. I know that I am intended to be more than I am, and I have always had a dream that I would have a Christian concert in my yard that was open to the public."

Find your voice and declare it. Allow the words to pass your lips and begin to create your future. Give yourself permission to say it out loud. Know that your order is being prepared and it will arrive when you are committed to it.

Six weeks later, she started a non-profit organization, Ignite Dubuque, where she hosted a concert in her yard for 1,500 people with Danny Gokey, from "American Idol," as the headliner.

Another example: During a Strategic Planning Session a client declared that they would go from \$200M/year to \$600M/year within the next 3 years. As they were saying it out loud, people in the room thought it was impossible and there was no way it was going to happen. Well, guess what? It's happened!

Like the Carnegie Hall story, when we speak about what we want to experience in our life, we create the space for things to begin to move. When you declare what you want, when you bring it into existence through language, and start saying yes to the things that help you achieve it, what you desire IS possible!

Declare Your Future! Be Focused! Be Fierce!

Questions:

What do you want to experience that makes you nervous to even say out loud?

What do you want your team or company to accomplish?

What is just outside your reach that you would be willing to go after?

CHAPTER FIVE

Aim For The Stars

Human beings are visual creatures. It's implanted into our DNA to do a large part of the processing of our world through the things we see. Sometimes we need a new perspective, especially when we're in too close. That's why I love the thought of zooming out, seeing the big picture and understanding how the pieces fit together.

For example, when I say "tropical vacation," what picture comes to mind? Do you see the letters V-A-C-A-T-I-0-N? Or do you see a mental image of a vacation? Do you see the simple letters or does your mind create the image of a beautiful tropical beach, complete with white sand, turquoise water and blue lounge chairs?

Of course, you see the image of the beach in your mind. Your image might not be exactly like mine, but they'd probably be close. Our minds naturally think in pictures and the better we can communicate the details of the picture, the more likely we are to achieve it.

Every organization needs someone to step up and be a visionary. Where there is no vision, the people perish (Proverbs 29:18). Whether that person wears the title of Coach, Founder, CEO, COO, CVO or President, the actual title doesn't really matter. Instead, what matters most is that there is someone on the team who can paint the picture, communicate the vision, and lead the team to accomplish something they have never accomplished before.

When I work with clients, we start by looking into the future to declare what they want to achieve. Once we have an idea of what we want to accomplish, we choose a date, determine a handful of key milestones that we'll need to pass and begin reverse engineering the roadmap until we end up at our current date. It's fun to watch teams create this together. Once that is complete, we begin putting in more details for the next 90 days of work.

I love the Michelangelo quote, "The greater danger for most of us lies not in setting our aim too high and falling short, but in setting our aim too low and achieving our mark." There's something about setting goals that helps our brain move into problem-solving mode.

I'm often asked, "Am I supposed to know how to accomplish the goals before I begin?" My answer might surprise you…Absolutely not! If we already knew how to achieve it, it would already be accomplished. The key is to…Suspend the How!

Suspend the How

When we are getting started on a new endeavor, we will automatically ask ourselves: How am I going to accomplish that? This is a terrible question because unless we've already done it, the answer our brain brings back is… I don't know and then we get stuck. We unintentionally create a barrier for ourselves and make it more difficult to get started.

You've probably heard the saying; "All the street lights don't have to be green before leaving the house." In other words, you know you're going to hit a red light from time to time, but you don't let that keep you in the driveway. You'll figure out how to handle the red lights when you get there.

So, if you're not finding the answer useful, the secret is to go back and ask yourself a better question: What is one step I could take to get started? Or, Given where I am now, what is one thing I could do to keep moving? By giving our mind a better question, we can decide what we want to do next. Once that step is accomplished we decide on the next step… rinse and repeat. By suspending the "how" you give yourself permission to move forward without knowing all the answers.

I hate to see people who get caught up in thinking too far down the road. When they can't see all the steps they're going to need to take, they decide that accomplishing their goal isn't possible after all and they back down without even taking the first step. I think Kris Kringle got it right when he sang…*Put one foot in front of the other, and soon you'll be walking cross the floor.*

The goal for the Competitive Show Choir was to go from nursing homes to Nationals, I had no idea how we were going to get there. I just knew that we had to improve our skills and keep aiming higher. When you start with a goal of "don't be last," the road to Nationals seems daunting and impossible. So, we laid out a roadmap that spanned several years and got clear about what we needed to accomplish each year. Then we put one foot in front of the other and got started.

Milestones:

Milestone 1: "We're not last!"

Our first milestone was, "Don't come in last!" You might laugh, but it took us a full two years just to accomplish that one. One of my favorite memories is getting on the bus after a full day of competing. I had the results in my hand and asked the students to quiet down so I could read the results out loud. I said, "The lowest scoring group today is"…and when I announced the team name, the bus erupted! It wasn't us! They began chanting, "We're not last! We're not last!" You would have thought that we had won the National Championship! I still laugh when I think about it. I mean, really. Who celebrates not being last? WE DID!

Check! What's the Next Step?

Milestone 2: Qualify for Night Finals in a competition. Each competition begins with all competing choirs performing in the day round. The choirs with the top 6 scores then make it to the second round: Night Finals.

It happened at Benton Community Touch of Class Competition. When the emcee announced that we had made night finals, our students went crazy. We were so excited and loud! Of course, I loved every minute of it. When the competition was finished, the director of the winning team came up and said, "Man, I wish my students were half as excited about winning as yours were about making night finals!" I remember his statement striking me as odd. They'd won the entire competition! How could they not be excited about that?

Check! What's the Next Step?

Milestone 3: <u>Qualify for Night Finals consistently</u>, which began to happen almost immediately. I could feel things beginning to tip; we were gaining momentum. Success was perpetuating and coming more quickly now. Incoming freshmen knew what I expected and in turn had high expectations for their own performance. They could feel the momentum and knew they'd have to work hard to continue the success.

Check! What's the Next Step?

Milestone 4: <u>Become the Grand Champion of a 3A Competition</u>

Check! What's the Next Step?

Milestone 5: <u>Compete in the Large School (4A) Category</u>

"Now that we'd won the title of Grand Champion at a small school competition, it's time to compete in the larger competitions." Competitions that attracted larger, powerhouse programs from Minneapolis, Cincinnati, and the Chicagoland area. We were going head to head with top notch performances and making night finals would be a stretch. It could have been a disaster, but we knew it was a necessary step to get where we ultimately wanted to go.

Check! What's the Next Step?

Milestone 6: <u>Make Night Finals in the Large School Division</u>. Iron Sharpens Iron. Being able to see those powerhouse shows helped us develop our skills. Now, we were among those staying and competing in the night finals while other schools two to three times larger than us were going home early. We were definitely beginning to make a name for ourselves.

Check! What's the Next Step?

Milestone 7: <u>Compete in the Large School Division in several states and win caption awards</u>. We competed in four different states: Minnesota, Wisconsin, Illinois, and our home state of Iowa. We were on a roll, winning caption awards like Best Vocals, Best Choreography, Best Band, Most Creative Show, Most Creative Costumes and Grand Champion.

Check! What's the Next Step?

Milestone 8: <u>Compete in a Small National Competition</u>. During our first national competition, the director from the Burbank (CA) Show Choir approached me and said, "I'm looking forward to seeing your group perform. I've heard some great things about you guys." After we performed, he found me again and said, "Wow! What a sound! Now I know why I've heard of you guys!" Burbank went on to win the competition and we came in third. It was wonderful! The kids were getting a taste of success on a much larger scale.

Check! What's the Next Step?

Milestone 9: <u>Compete in a Large National Competition</u>. We traveled to Nashville, TN, which was a long 10.5 hours ride in a couple of busses to compete at Show Choir Nationals, a competition known for attracting the best of the best. We had 60 students and were followed out there by about 100 fans. What a great trip! We had a blast and our performance was fantastic! The competition was amazing and the shows we got to see at the competition were spectacular.

Like all Show Choir Competitions, the day round is used to discover the top six shows that will perform again that night. We came in seventh, so we didn't make it to the night round, which was disappointing. We felt like we did our best and it's always easier to lose when you know you've left your best out on the field.

Although we lost the "war," there was another, more personal, battle that we were paying attention to. Throughout the year we had gone head-to-head with a school from the Chicagoland area. We would win one competition, then they would win the next. We went back and forth throughout the year going up against each other at four different competitions. We were going into the National Competition tied for wins. They had won two Grand Championships; we had won two Grand Championships. Show Choir Nationals would be the tie-breaker.

When I announced that we had placed higher than our rivals, the room erupted in energetic cheering. I think this illuminates the fact that people want to be on a winning team; even when we lose, we still look for the win.

It took 13 years of consistent growth to go from "Don't come in last" to placing seventh at Show Choir Nationals in Nashville, TN. Looking back, our journey was marked with a long list of accomplished goals. It was fun being part of the journey where we were all growing and becoming something far more than we could've ever imagined when we first started out.

There's a verse in the Bible that says, "Do not despise these small beginnings..." (Zechariah 4:10 NLT) Everything great begins as something small. Sometimes so small that you can't even see it...like an idea or a dream. When I started out, competing at a national competition was so far in the future I couldn't even see it. But setting specific, ambitious goals built on the goals achieved from the year before brought us closer and closer with each passing year. It was intentional work, and we made it…From Nursing Homes to Nationals.

Setting Strong Goals

Whenever I tell clients that we're going to set some meaningful and measurable goals, there is almost always an audible groan in the room, lots of eye rolling accompanied by an almost palpable "Oh no. Not this again" vibe. I can almost hear their inner chatter hitting warp speed: I don't have enough information to set a goal. I don't know what goal I'd set. What if I set a goal and fail. I've already got a plan I don't need a goal. Who is she to say I need a goal. I don't have to listen to her. This is stupid.

Even though people logically know that goals are useful, they resist setting them because of the chatter they've become entangled with and most of the time, the chatter isn't even true.

Many of us may dream of success in some area of our life, which is a good beginning, but not enough. Napoleon Hill said, "Goals are dreams with deadlines." There's something about the deadline that engages the goal-achieving machine part of our brain.

I encourage my clients to set three goals at a time. Three goals seem just about right. It's a manageable number, not too many and not too few. Plus, I love the phrase, *omne trium perfectum,* which means, "Everything that comes in threes is perfect." Sometimes I might agree to a different number, but three is the sweet spot I highly encourage.

Goals are like magnets; the things we set goals about are the things that attract our attention and resources. They give the chance to:

- Identify the key areas that will have the biggest impact on achieving what we want to experience in our lives.
- Remain focused and avoid being distracted by the things that are urgent yet rarely important.
- Make intelligent decisions about how to spend our time and resources.

Make Them Behavior-Based

Many people use the acronym SMART to describe the kind of goals they want to set: Specific, Measurable, Achievable (or Aligned if you're working with a team of people), Realistic and Timely.

I like using the formula:

(Insert verb) (Insert what you're focused on) from _____ to _____ by (Insert date).

Example: Increase stock turns from four to eight by December 31

Example: Increase our customer satisfaction score from 82 to 95 by December 31.

Example: Decrease my weight from 170 to 140 pounds by April 30.

I was working with a big insurance company whose leadership wanted me to help the sales team increase their performance. I asked the group, "What goals do you have in place?" A member of the team perked up and confidently offered, "I have a goal. My goal is to achieve $4.2M in new sales." I replied, "That's a great place to start. Your final sales number is a fantastic lag measure. What goals do you have for the behaviors you'll focus on that will give you a predictable way to hit your sales number?" She looked at me as if I had grown another head.

I explained that achieving $4.2M in new sales will be fantastic but focusing on the number wasn't going to help her achieve that goal. Achieving $4.2M in new sales will be the result of successful, behavior-based goal setting. We got curious about all the actions that she could focus on and then through the process of elimination narrowed the list down to 3 areas of focus. She set SMART goals for those specific behaviors, giving her predictable indicators to monitor and measure her progress throughout the rest of the year.

As it turns out, she knocked it out of the park, achieved her $4.2M in new sales and qualified to receive her entire bonus.

Side note: Two people in that initial goal-setting meeting thought that simply having a sales quota was enough. They went to their HR Department and requested permission to leave the class saying: I've already got this. I already know about goal setting. This is a waste of my time. She's never sold insurance so what could she teach me? Being un-coachable can really bite people in the backside. Guess who didn't hit their sales quota and didn't earn their bonus?

Always Room To Grow

You've probably heard the saying before but it bears repeating…Life is not about the destination; it's about the journey. The beauty of goal setting is found in the process of experiencing who we need to become in order to achieve the goal. It's the process that prepares us, refines us, gets us ready for whatever is next and reflects back to us what we believe about ourselves. We must become someone we've never been in order to achieve something we've never achieved.

This is the beauty of infinite potential. We will forever be growing, developing, reaching, changing and achieving. Even when you think you've arrived at the summit, there will be another magnificent mountain to climb.

I thought that aiming for Nationals was lofty, only to be surprised by a letter I received 4 weeks before I left teaching. The envelope was made from heavily bonded ivory paper. It looked like a fancy wedding invitation. I didn't recognize the return address, so I tore it open wondering what was inside.

I read the calligraphy script headline, "Dubuque Wahlert Impulse, under the direction of Pamela Mumm, has been pre-qualified to compete." The script continued, "Because of your outstanding competition history and the high caliber of your choir's performance, the International Organizing Committee has reviewed and granted you qualification for Championship Competition, the highest level of participation in the World Choir Games. I personally hope you will help represent the very best of American Show Choir to the rest of the world."

As I read, then re-read the invitation, I felt all those competitive juices begin to flow again. The goal of reaching nationals had been achieved and now here was an opportunity to go to the next level and compete internationally. I had to remind myself that this desire had served its purpose and run its course. I was leaving teaching and starting a new chapter in my professional life. Competing internationally would be a possibility for the next director.

Going from nursing homes to Nationals seemed like an unattainable goal when we started. We identified the milestones that would help us keep track of our progress. With each milestone, we found more opportunities to create memorable experiences.

Set Worthy and Winnable Goals! Be Focused! Be Fierce!

Questions

- How would achieving these goals affect your life?
- How would achieving these goals affect the people you love?
- What are actions you could start monitoring to let you know you're headed in the right direction?

CHAPTER SIX

The Hardest Step

Early on in the morning of August 7, 1974, a 24-year old French performance artist named Philippe Petit took his very first step on the 1-inch cable that stretched between the Twin Towers of the World Trade Center in New York City.

It was a dream Petit called "le Coup" and it had been 6 years in the making. When Petit first arrived in New York City, he emerged from the subway tunnel to get his first view of the Towers. "Like a slap in the face I saw that my dream was impossible." But he made his way into the Towers and sneaked to the upper floors, which were still under construction at the time. He climbed the unfinished stairway to the rooftop and looked across the 130-ft expanse to the other tower before making his way back down to the plaza below. Only now, looking back up to the top of the towers did the walk look like it might actually be possible.

For the next 8 months, Petit practiced, planned, dreamed, and strategized. He would get frustrated and abandon the project only to go back to it days later with renewed focus. Petit says that the more he got to know the towers the more they became an ally. "They became my friends." He was becoming more and more familiar with the idea of achieving his dream.

Finally the day was upon him. It took Petit and a couple of accomplices all night long to rig the wire and get it properly secured between the towers. At a little after 7:00 in the morning Petit took his first step out onto the wire, 1,350 feet off the ground.

"My left foot was on the wire. My right foot and the weight of my body was anchored to the solidity of the tower. Without asking me, my right leg went on the wire. And here I was walking." He had visualized and practiced that step so many times that by the time he was actually there, the foot moved on its own without a conscious thought.

Remembering that first step, Petit says, "When I found myself one foot on the wire, one foot on the building and ready to decide to shift my weight to become a bird, it was not something new. And after a few steps I knew I was in my element."

Today Petit says, "You need dreams to live. It's as essential as a road to walk on and bread to eat. I would have felt myself dying if this dream would have been taken away from me by reason. The dream was as big as the towers. It was really anchored to me in such a way that life was not conceivable without doing this."

Sound familiar? Can you identify with Petit? Do you have dreams that are so anchored inside you that you can't conceive of life without pursuing those dreams? The sad thing is that so many wonderful dreams are left unrealized; they never come true because they're never pursued. No plans are made, no strategies laid out, no steps taken to see that the dreams are given a chance to become more than just dreams.

Start!

How many projects, plans, businesses, relationships, or opportunities haven't even seen the light of day because they were never started? The dream was conceived in the mind, but then the chatter with thoughts of fear or insecurity or the lack of confidence sneaks in and disrupts the dream causing it to die before it ever gets off the ground.

So how do you move from the dream stage to the implementation stage without getting stuck? How do you jump-start yourself before the dream loses momentum and dies away? How do you get moving forward in the right direction?

There are several reasons why folks get stuck before taking the first step toward the fulfillment of their dreams. The first reason is because they don't have a good view of the road all the way through to success. Or to put it another way, people don't take the first step because they think they need to see all the rest of the steps of the project clearly before they start.

It's human nature to want to see how the steps are arranged before starting. We see the first step and maybe even the next two or three steps. But we don't see how those steps could be enough and it causes us to shrink back. We don't trust that we'll be able to figure out steps four, five, and six after we've taken steps one, two, and three.

Like big pavers of a sidewalk directed toward your goal, you don't need to worry about where that eighth paver will go until you get to number seven. Remember, your perspective will change every time you take a step. Don't worry that you don't have all the steps figured out. Just start moving and take the first step!

You'd be surprised how many of my clients timidly take their first step only to look back days or weeks later and be surprised by how much they've accomplished.

Remember Your Future

Often people don't get started because they don't understand how important their future is. They can't picture it in their minds. Let me encourage you with this…you and your future are important to this world. I know that statement seems obvious, but I want to make sure you're getting it. Your future is vastly more important than your past. It's so important that it will wait for you.

One of the most valuable tools I learned was remembering your future. I know that remembering something that hasn't happened yet doesn't seem to make much sense, but stay with me. I learned this lesson when I invited my mentor to town to speak at my first No Excuses Conference. I was tense the night before the event was to begin. I was distracted and my stomach was in knots about the various details surrounding the event.

My mentor, Paul Martinelli, saw my state of anxiety and gave me just the right words at just the right time. He told me, "Pam, this is a time for you to remember your future." Of course, I had no idea what he meant by that. He caught my expression and explained, "Imagine tomorrow. See yourself on the stage. See the audience responding to you, raising their hands, engaging with each other. See it flawlessly in your mind. Now, tomorrow all you are doing is bringing to life the things you've already imagined."

I've always known that visualization is important. But I've usually thought of it as a sports thing. Like the high jumper who imagines herself arching beautifully over the bar before she even takes a step. The successful jump began in her mind before it was ever realized. But what I learned is that visualization is important in many other ways as well.

A trip to Paris isn't complete without a visit to the famous Louvre art museum. You enter through the modern glass pyramid, which leads to three separate wings. You make your way to the Denon Wing and as you pause to look up you notice the grand painted ceilings, reminding you that before it was a museum, the Louvre was a palace, home to some of Europe's mightiest kings.

You continue through Denon Wing and follow the crowd to Room 6, where you find one of Leonardo da Vinci's most famous works, the *Mona Lisa*. You're almost taken aback. You've seen so many pictures of this painting in books; you've seen reproductions on placemats, posters and even t-shirts.

But now you find yourself standing in front of the one and only original. But is this painting really the original portrait of Mona Lisa?

No, it's not. The version found in the Louvre in Paris is actually the first replica. The original was painted on the canvas in Leonardo's mind. He visualized what it would look like. He pictured the colors he'd use, the surface he'd paint on, even the pose he would ask the woman to strike. The painting was composed one brush stroke at a time, until the image in his mind was brought into the world. I love the thought of remembering or imagining the future before it happens.

I will use this technique with clients as they are preparing for cold calls, conversations with colleagues, family members and customer service agents. The key is to remember to use this technique prior to the experience.

So where is your focus today? Where your focus goes, your energy flows. Just like whatever you think about gets bigger. If you're constantly dwelling on your past by going back again and again to mistakes that were made, then you can expect your past to loom large in your mind, giving it more power in the present and future than it deserves.

You bring power to your future by being future-minded, thinking and dreaming about what is to come. I call it being in a "toward state" rather than an "away state." It's like constantly blaming circumstances or people from your past for your present status. That's exactly the kind of thinking that sucks all the energy away from your present and future. It's the kind of thinking that drains you instead of inspires you.

The future is yours to co-create, experience and shape the way you want it to be. Create a life filled with happiness, health, love and full self-expression. You were designed to accomplish great things. Be the light in your own life and shine brightly on others.

Get Started! Be Focused! Be Fierce!

Questions:

What have you created on the canvas of your mind that you will be remembering in your future?

What will you start experiencing today?

What fearful thoughts are releasing you from their grip?

CHAPTER SEVEN

The Health of the Relationship

We all know that no one achieves anything great in life all alone, which means that in order to accomplish anything significant we have to work with other people. And as we are working with other people it is important to keep the health of a relationship in mind. One of the most important relationships in my life is the relationship with my parents and, specifically, with my father.

As I mentioned earlier, I have always been Daddy's little girl. When something good, bad, or ugly happens, I want to tell my dad all about it. Even now, I talk with my dad almost every day. Sometimes it's to have a political discussion, sometimes it's to get an update on the week and sometimes it's for practical things like how do I start my snow blower…a conversation we have every single winter.

I do not like thinking about it, but my greatest fear is who will I be when my parents are no longer living. My relationship with them is an anchor in my life. I rely on them for that grounding conversation every single week. They are the people in my life who actively ask me how things are going. They make time for me whenever I pop in and they are the people I can lean on in any situation, no matter what. Who will I be when they are no longer here? My dad's health has provided many opportunities for me to think about this.

When Tragedy Teaches a Lesson

My dad's health issues began innocently enough. The children in the family were outside jumping on the trampoline and my dad decided to join the fun. Not only did he join, he decided to attempt a back flip. We were all around the perimeter of the trampoline, cheering him on and I was the designated camera operator to make sure there would be proof of the accomplishment.

The video shows him bouncing, giving it all he has. He springs up and begins to arch his back, bring his legs up over his head and as if it was in slow motion, his momentum stopped, literally in mid-air, and he came down landing on the back of his neck. At first, I laughed and then quickly realized something was wrong.

He managed to get himself to the side of the trampoline and onto the ground. We loaded him up and took him to the nearest hospital. They decided it was a "football stinger" and sent us home. After 3 days of remaining in constant pain, my mom took him back to a hospital in our area. They took x-rays and the doctor on call, who happened to be my mom's doctor, called and said, "First, turn off your stove. Second, your husband is OK but we found a hairline fracture in his neck. We've immobilized his neck and have scheduled surgery." It was alarming to think he'd been walking around for three days with a broken neck!

During the surgery, the spinal cord was nicked, causing fluid to leak and required Dad to spend the next five days flat on his back, healing. To cheer him up, we were given permission to bring his 5 lb. Yorkshire Terrier named Precious to visit him. It was wonderful to see his spirits lift.

Thank you, God…

In 1998, while sitting around the kitchen table with my family, my world screeched to a halt. My eyes were dripping, my ears ringing, and my mind was racing. I couldn't see, hear or think. Did I just hear my dad correctly? Did he just say "lung cancer?"

During a routine checkup, my dad told his doctor that his joints were aching, he'd lost a lot of weight and wondered if the doctor would do a chest x-ray. Luckily, the doctor agreed to the test and found a dark spot on my dad's right lung. Surgery was scheduled and the doctors told my dad that if the cancer was in the lymph nodes there was nothing they could do and they would simply sew him up. My dad said, "Well in that case, I hope I wake up in pain." The early detection helped, the cancer had not spread, the surgeon removed 2 lobes from his right lung to make sure they got all the cancerous tissue and the surgery went well.

Thank you, God...

His post-op therapy called for intense chemotherapy treatments. Two days after his final round of chemo, my dad's intestines ruptured and he was rushed back to the hospital for more surgery. He left the hospital with a colostomy bag, a long recovery process in front of him, and finishing with a procedure to remove the bag.

Thank you, God...

A couple of years after recovering from lung cancer, dad was preparing for deer season. He remembers sitting on a log, holding his head trying to figure out why he was in the woods and why all the leaves around him had been swept away. He looked up, saw the deer stand, and realized that while he was tightening the safety strap, the stand swung around, hit him on the head and he had fallen off the 16 foot ladder.

He was in pain, confused, disoriented and had lost his glasses. He knew where he parked, but he couldn't remember how to get there. He started walking and eventually found his truck...blackout...he began driving and came to a T-intersection. He tried to turn his head, nothing happened, he could only move his eyeballs and slowly began to pull out on the road...blackout... he was driving on the interstate (he never takes the interstate home from his hunting spot) and wondered, what am I doing here?...blackout...6 hours after falling off the ladder, he walked in the house...

After all those years of marriage, Mom knew at a glance that something was wrong. Dad said, "I think I broke my neck." Mom immediately grabbed her keys and they headed to the emergency room where x-rays showed that nothing was wrong.

Four days later Dad was still not quite himself. His neck hurt, and he still couldn't turn his head, so he went back to the hospital. The x-ray tech gave him some weights to hold in each hand and when the results came back, he had broken six vertebrae in his neck. Needless to say, he was admitted and surgery was scheduled. I know... what are the chances that finding nothing wrong could happen 2 times and be wrong both times?

Thank you, God…

Later we hiked back to the spot where he fell out of the tree. You could see where a circle, about 12 feet in diameter, of leaves, limbs, and dirt had been disturbed. He had rolled around for hours before being able to walk. And yes, we found his glasses.

In 2009, dad was going in for his final cancer checkup and during the MRI they found another spot. The lung cancer came back with a vengeance. It was in his left lung AND his lymph nodes. When he heard lymph nodes, naturally, he thought nothing could be done. Luckily, he was wrong. Due to the significant developments in cancer research, they were able to remove the lymph nodes and instead of taking out an entire lobe of lung, only removed a wedge of tissue.

Thank you, God…

Again, there was a regiment of chemotherapy treatments following the surgery and after the 2nd infusion, he was out playing golf with his grandchildren, Garrett and Gabrielle. He thought he had pulled a muscle in his back and laid down on the 7th green. He went to the doctor and found out that he'd had a heart attack. His triple bypass surgery was on June 22. I remember the date, because it was my birthday. We had all made it to the hospital to be together as a family. We had each taken turns hugging him and giving him encouraging words before the orderlies came to take him into the operating room. We had no sooner gotten to the waiting room when a nurse came running in, telling me that I needed to follow her immediately.

As we hurried down the hall, my mind whirled with the puzzling possibilities. What is going on? What's wrong? Why didn't he ask for my mother?

I followed the nurse into a pre-op area. I could tell by looking at my father that he was already starting to get a little loopy. As soon as he saw me, he started singing "Happy Birthday" and through slurred words he told me that he loved me. Of course, I began to cry! Like I said, I'm daddy's little girl.

Thank you, God…

2014 My dad was diagnosed with lung cancer for the third time. A spot of cancer was found in the left lung and more concerning was the inoperable tumor that had grown around the aorta and esophagus. Once again, cancer research had improved and between the ability to use pinpoint radiation and chemo, the doctor felt confident that removing the cancer was possible. He prepared himself for the road ahead. Every day for 6 weeks he went in for the 8 rounds of chemo and 30 rounds of radiation treatment.

Thank you, God…today Dad is Cancer Free!

To me, my dad is a remarkable man. He's been blessed with an amazing opportunity not just to be a cancer survivor but to be a cancer thriver: He and my mom have been active in the Relay for Life raising over $200K for cancer research. He's the President of the Independence, Iowa Faternal Order of Eagles #4544 and active in the Independence Presbyterian Church.

I know that one day, he will no longer be around, but that day isn't today. My friend Barry always says, "Never mourn the living." So, instead of focusing on the fear, the worry and the sadness, I am focused on building the relationship I want with my dad while he is alive.

The Last Five Conversations

I have the privilege of teaching "Foundations," authored by Paul Axtel with my colleague Pamela Hillary. Whenever we teach the section on relationships, I share the story of my father and how important it is to gauge the health of a relationship. Paul says: An easy way to determine the health of any relationship is to look at the last five conversations you had with that person.

If those conversations were superficial, trivial check-ins, then there is an opportunity to deepen the relationship. Parents' minds will often drift to the conversations they have with their children. Did you do your homework? Did you brush your teeth? Are you ready for bed? Do you need a ride? What time do you need to be picked up? What time will you be home?

When they start to look at the depth of those conversations, they realize that while those conversations are necessary, there is an opportunity to elevate the skills that could deepen the relationships.

I realized that when my dad was going through each of these events, I was asking questions like, "What time is your next doctor's appointment?" "Do you want me to go with you?" "What medicines are you on?" "What would you like for dinner?" "What time do you want to eat?" "Did you do your breathing exercises?" "Did you take your pills?" These questions showed my concern, but they were all superficial and safe. They were questions that kept emotions at arms distance.

I decided to change the relationship by changing the questions I was asking. I started to ask: "What are you concerned about?" "What happened this week?" "What's going on with your health?" "How do you think your body is handling the medicine?" "What are you concerned about?" I was getting better at asking questions, and then I felt like I had an epiphany, if our brain is a goal-achieving machine, wouldn't it make sense to ask questions that would help my dad find confirmation that his body is healing and getting stronger? I started asking, "What feels better today?" "What's feeling stronger?" "What can you do today that would have been a struggle last week?"

Listening

As important as questions are, they are only half of the equation. The other half is the skill of listening and not just staying silent and pretend listening, but actually listening and listening generously. Most of the time people listen through filters. Filters to determine whether they agree or disagree with what is being said. A filter to determine whether the information is right or wrong. A filter to determine what we will say next or how what they are saying relates to us.

Listening generously is the most under-utilized skill that people have at their fingertips. Instead we judge the words, the ideas, the delivery, the tone, the inflection, the timing, etc... We get so distracted by our own thinking that we forget to simply listen. Listening to understand, listening to hear what they are committed to and listening to strengthen the connection.

My favorite listening formula has 3 parts:

> Part 1: Let them know what you heard them say
>
> Part 2: Identify what you think they are feeling
>
> Part 3: Acknowledge the greater good that they are trying to achieve

Listening is one of the greatest gifts we can give to the people we love and care about. The more we listen, the more people perceive that we care about them and people will speak to the level that we are willing to listen.

When we are able to listen and keep the focus on the person speaking, they are able to express what they want to say without feeling like they've been hijacked or dominated. I like to call this "curiosity-based listening." When we are listening, instead of thinking about what we are going to say, or what we want to tell them about ourselves, we listen and ask at least one question that allows the person speaking to expand on some aspect of their experience.

Just by changing the questions and listening to my dad's answers, I was able to change the depth of our relationship. It wasn't enough to just use words; I had a desire for a more meaningful relationship with the man who has been important in my life since the day I was born. I've always loved my dad and this awareness simply allowed our relationship to become something that it hadn't been before. It allowed me to show up in a way that I hadn't shown up before.

Relationships matter. Whether it's the relationship with our parents, siblings, friends, spouse, or children or it's the relationship we have with our coworkers, peers, boss, or direct reports, it's relationships that give life meaning. I used to take relationships for granted. I would blow people off, not really pay attention, show up late, and disregard what they needed or wanted.

Now I realize that when I intentionally build healthy relationships I get to experience the full tapestry of our life.

Build Healthy Relationships! Be Focused! Be Fierce!

Questions:

What relationships do you have that could use some attention?

What question could you ask to add depth to the relationship?

Where could listening generously help a relationship?

CHAPTER EIGHT

Deal With Ourselves First

When I begin working with clients, they will often say that they want to be a better leader. They will read books, listen to podcasts, talk with mentors, sign up to receive a done-for-you template, and then become frustrated when none of these things solve their problem. I see this time and time again, and what I've found is that in order to master the external world, you must first become a master of your inner world.

Let's start this chapter with a thought exercise: Have you ever wondered what it would be like to feel fully empowered, confident and prepared regardless of the situation or circumstance you found yourself encountering? That you would be calm and confident regardless of what another person said or what another person did? That you were unstoppable because you were so tuned in to your own thinking that nothing and no one could disrupt you from your game?

I have found that nothing can throw me off my game as quickly as interacting with other people. Don't get me wrong. I love people, they just always seem to be around when I'm not at my best.

Here's a story when I was definitely not at my best, and if life extended mulligans, I would definitely request a do-over.

The List Goes Up

After doing her best at her show choir audition, Belle (not her real name) anxiously scanned the list looking for her name. Going into her junior year, she anticipated being a part of the Varsity Show Choir. Unfortunately, her skills had not progressed and she found herself placed on the Prep Show Choir team.

Of course she wanted to be on the Varsity Show Choir team with her friends, but she absolutely could not match pitch…she couldn't carry a tune. This wasn't an issue when she was a freshman or even a sophomore. There was always plenty of grace at that level of the program. But to be accepted onto the competitive varsity team, the minimum, absolute minimum requirement was the ability to match pitch.

Sounds logical...right?

Belle's Mom Attacks

Well, "logical" wasn't going to cut it with Belle's mom. I still remember the first parent-teacher conference following that decision. Belle's mother sat across the table from me asking why her daughter wasn't chosen to be a part of the Varsity Show Choir. Like Belle, her mother made the assumption that her seniority in the program would predict her automatic advancement to the Varsity group along with her peers.

The mother was in full-on damage control. She was dealing with a disappointed daughter and was desperate for options. What did she need to do to ensure her daughter would make the Varsity Show Choir next time tryouts came around?

As I sat across from the mother, I explained very carefully what her daughter would need to do to make the Varsity group as a senior. I told her that Belle had a hard time matching pitch, and since this is a competitive choir, that was the minimum requirement for acceptance. I gave her the names of private instructors and suggested that she take private voice lessons to sharpen her skills.

Belle was a good dancer but without the ability to match pitch, the show choir was not the place for her. Dancing without singing is called a Dance Team, and I encouraged her to try out for that group, thinking that it would be a better seat on the bus for Belle's natural talent. I told mom in no uncertain terms that if Belle couldn't match pitch, she would not make the Varsity Show Choir her senior year.

But Belle's mother kept pushing. She wasn't satisfied and wasn't hearing what I was saying. She persisted with the point that, "There are no competitive guidelines about the size of the group. Why can't you just make the group bigger so Belle could be a part of it?" With her voice escalating, she continued, "For goodness sakes! She can't stay in the Prep group. That group is for freshmen and sophomores. My daughter is a junior and she's embarrassed to be left behind while her friends move up."

I was trying to explain my commitment to making the show choir the very best it could be, and after a full 20 minutes of tip-toeing around the issue, I blurted out, "I'm sorry, but I could expand the group to a hundred students and your daughter would still not be on the team. She lacks the skills required to be a part of this group."

What a zinger...that comment certainly shut her up. The color drained from her face until she turned beat red with anger, got up, left the table and continued with her other parent-teacher meetings.

The Moment of Truth

The next year rolled around. Belle was a senior and it was time to try out. I had been talking with Belle throughout the year and knew that she had been taking private voice lessons. I was curious to hear how she'd progressed and was looking forward to her audition. The minute she opened her mouth to sing, my heart sank. She had made progress but definitely not enough to be in the top competitive choir.

As I listened to her sing, I knew I absolutely could not put this girl into the Varsity Show Choir. But in a moment of weakness, I caved. After all, she was pleasant, likable, a good dancer and her peers enjoyed her. I made the decision to put Belle in the group.

I foolishly believed that just one person, all by herself, wouldn't be able to undermine what the group was going to accomplish that year.

From Bad to Worse

As we started into rehearsals that year, I could tell something wasn't right. I wondered why the alto part was so off. What is going on? I did my best to zero in on the problem. I had the various parts sing by themselves. Every section sounded great. But when we put it together, something was terribly off.

The more I worked with them, the more frustrated I became, and worse, I could tell the students were getting frustrated too. I could see it in their faces, "Why do we have to go over and over this?"

After one particularly frustrating rehearsal, one of the young men from the choir came up and asked if he could talk with me privately. "Sure," I said. "What's on your mind?" His words still make my stomach churn. "You keep getting mad at us because we're not singing the correct parts. But the problem is my partner, Belle. She's terrible. She's okay when she's alone but as soon as the other parts start, she's way off."

Oh no, I thought. What have I done?

As the young man walked away, I took a deep breath. Okay, maybe it's not that bad. I thought back to her audition...it wasn't that bad, was it? And wasn't she still working hard on her lessons? Maybe we could pull this together after all, I thought, as I tried to ignore the inevitable mess staring me in the face.

To reassure myself, I reached out to her private vocal coach and asked how the lessons were going. He laughed and said that as soon as she found out she made the Varsity Show Choir, she quit the lessons. I was stunned. What was she thinking? She had the opportunity to get better, but she was choosing to remain terrible.

Making the Most of a Bad Situation

It was time to address the situation directly. No more tip-toeing around the situation. It was not going to just magically disappear. I was going to have to step up, stare the problem in the face and do something.

I was going to take control of the things I could control. And her participation in the choir was something I could control. I pulled Belle aside for a heart-to-heart conversation to discuss the options:

Option 1: I could insist that she pick her lessons back up. She hadn't completed what she promised, and I could require her to fulfill her commitment and go back to her lessons. It may not make things better, but at least it would show her commitment to getting better.

Option 2: She could save face and stay in the group, but I would have to insist that she not sing. It was like the episode of Andy Griffith where Barney was off pitch so they kept asking him to sing softer and softer and softer until he was inaudible. It was funny in the episode, but I found no humor having to deal with this in real life.

Option 3: I could kick her out of the group. After quitting the lessons, she certainly deserved it. She'd deceived me, and the group, by doing only what was necessary to get into the choir but not doing enough to actually help the team.

Belle chose Option 1. In addition to the lessons, we identified the parts of the set where she could hear her part and was able to match the pitch. During those parts, she would sing the alto part. Then we identified the parts of the show where she wasn't able to hear the harmony, and those would be the times she would either sing the melody or pull a "Barney Fife" and simply mouth the words.

I was not happy with myself at all. Given the situation, it was an adequate solution, but it was a sharp contrast to what it could've been if I'd done the right thing when I was deciding who had the skills to be in the group.

The Lessons Learned

Somehow, in my youthful ignorance, I believed that the problem was Belle. She couldn't match pitch. She stopped taking lessons. She was an under-performer. Her mom is persistent…(and scary)!

I was getting frustrated, why couldn't anyone see how hard this was for me? I was the victim. If she had done what she said she was going to do, everything would have been fine.

I hear similar patterns when I work with people today. It's easy to target and blame the situation, an individual or a team for the problem: The team needs to take more ownership. The team needs to step up. The team needs to be more responsible. (Name) never follows through.

And yet, the entire situation happened because of my poor leadership. The team was in this position because of a decision that I made. I decided who would and would not be on the team. I decided how I would or would not handle the situation. I decided what conversations I would or would not have. The decisions that I made were what set things in motion.

Let's go back to the interaction with Belle's mom. I said, "I'm sorry, but I could expand the group to a hundred students and your daughter would still not be on the team. She lacks the skills required to a part of this group."

The problem actually happened when I thought that her mother shouldn't have been upset. I thought she should see this from my perspective and understand. I made my comment out of frustration and then felt bad because I'd been too harsh. I wanted to avoid another awkward and direct conversation with her mother, so I caved. I put Belle in the group hoping and praying that everything would work out. I made the decision out of guilt and avoidance.

I thought Belle wouldn't be able to handle the results of my decision. I made assumptions that Belle would fall apart, that her group of peers would be mad that she didn't make the team, or that her mother would be angry and I'd have to go through that whole ugly situation all over again. Likewise, I assumed that her mother wouldn't be able to handle the results of my decision either and that she'd start speaking poorly about me, telling people in the community that I was a bad teacher, etc.

Instead of focusing on the skills that were necessary from each participant so the group could succeed at the highest level, I began focusing on the things that I was making up about the situation and worse, I made a decision based on the things that I was making up about the situation.

In the process of being the weakest link, I did 3 damaging things:

- I put a specific individual in a situation where she would likely fail.

- I put a team of people in a situation where they were not at their best.
- I put my own credibility in jeopardy.

Making Decisions Based on Stories

How often do we make decisions based on what we are making up rather than on reality?

During a workshop, a National Sales Director started talking about a regional sales manager that reports to him. He was sharing that his team wasn't using the CRM (Customer Relationship Management) software, business was being left on the table, and he was frustrated that the team wasn't performing at the level necessary for success.

Okay, the regional sales manager was underperforming. Everyone on the team knew it, but the fact was, no one was addressing the issue. As we continued to talk about it, he said that he didn't want to appear too harsh, unfair, or intimidating. He didn't want to appear like a tyrant or a micromanager.

Are you starting to hear it? This national sales manager was making up stories. He was making up the story that people would see him as a tyrant. He was making up the story that people would think he was unfair. As a result, he thought that addressing the situation directly would make him appear intimidating.

I had to laugh because it was so clear to me that no one would ever consider him too harsh, direct or intimidating. People in the organization were actually talking about what a pushover he was! The team could see that the regional sales director was not doing his job and there were no consequences for the poor performance.

But his perspective, his stories, kept him stuck in place. The things he was making up in his mind were causing him to approach the situation from a weakened position. By not holding himself accountable to show up as a person who had the capacity to deal with the regional sales manager, he was losing credibility with the team. Frustration, anger, stress, and confusion were all setting in. All because he blindly believed that the issue was the regional sales manager.

Isn't it amazing how clearly we can see what is happening in a situation when it involves others, but when it's our situation, we are blind to our own shortcomings. As you were reading the story of Belle, I'm sure you were able to see my missteps. I messed up by putting her on the team. I messed up by turning a blind eye. I messed up by trying to solve it as a group issue rather than an individual issue.

Had I dealt with myself and the stories I was making up before I posted the list, all of this would have been avoided. By turning a blind eye (or more to the point, a deaf ear!) to Belle's participation, I was acting in direct conflict with our stated goal of being named "Grand Champion." I was acting in direct conflict with who I wanted to be as a teacher and a leader. I had an opportunity to reveal what I stood for, and instead I chose the path that ended with a lame second best solution.

A Leader's Clear Focus

It's always easier to see things in the lives of others rather than see things in our own life. This is why I'm such a big fan of observational learning. When we hear other people talk about their situations, we are able to see the parallels to our own life and then make the necessary course corrections to achieve what we want to experience.

As I continue working with people, I've learned that it's not my responsibility to develop the talent in others. You heard me right. I don't believe it is my responsibility to develop the talent in others. I believe it's their job to develop their own talent. My job is to develop the talents within me that ultimately amplify the talents in others. My job is to see others as perfectly resourced, whole human beings who are capable of living an adult life. I am responsible for my thinking, I'm accountable for my action, and it's on me to make sure I remove myself from any disempowered state that has me believing that it's OK to be a victim.

They are responsible for their thinking, they are accountable for their actions and it is on them to remove themselves from any disempowered state that has them believing it's OK to be a victim.

This concept doesn't always sit well with everyone. Some people believe that other people are empty vessels and it is their job, as a mentor/boss/employer/family member/friend/parent or sibling, to fill them up and pour all their wisdom into them. We secretly believe that they need our help, that they can't handle it by themselves and that we need to rescue them from the station.

The opportunity that's available to all of us when we're working with other people is to support the person who is the owner of that talent, to encourage them, give feedback when needed, put them in situations where that talent can be developed, and amplify the genius that's already inside them.

We are constantly dealing with a variety of situations and people. We are constantly making decisions about who will move up, who will be put on special projects, who will have more responsibility, who is falling behind, who has more seniority, even who will be let go. These decisions are all necessary, but the most important thing we bring to the situation is a clear, focused mind.

Being good stewards of the roles we have within an organization, we must keep in mind that we are responsible for the thoughts we bring to every situation. When we forget to be the expert at being us, we become the weakest link and people will not be able to thrive under our leadership. As leaders we have an enormous responsibility. We must be willing to pay attention to reality, be rigorous with accountability and consistently elevate our own level of awareness.

It's easy to fall into the temptation to make decisions based on our insecurities or feelings (like guilt) or the things we make up about a situation. But when we can maintain a rigorous focus on our goals, focus on the facts rather than the fictional interpretation we are creating, we'll find that it's much easier to make intelligent decisions.

I think The Fray got it right in their song entitled, "All at Once," when they sang, "Sometimes the hardest thing and the right thing are the same."

Mind Your Thoughts! Be Focused! Be Fierce!

Questions:

1) When you find yourself in a state of upset, what stories are you making up?

2) When you're in that story, what actions do you end up taking?

3) When you take those actions, how often are you dissatisfied with the results?

CHAPTER NINE

Giving Gratefully

In 2011, I walked into the first session of the John Maxwell Conference along with 500 leaders and entrepreneurs from all over the world. As a teacher, I had been applying the Maxwell material in my classroom for years, but on that day, I was entering the room as a Founding Member of the John Maxwell Training Team.

The Maxwell Team talked a lot about giving back throughout the conference. They talked about tithing, which is the practice of giving 10% of your income back to God. They taught that tithing wasn't something we owed to God but rather something we gratefully give back to Him. In the book, *The Science of Getting Rich*, Wallace Wattles writes, "As you go in the Certain Way, opportunities will come to you in increasing numbers; and you will need to be very steady in your faith and purpose, and to keep in close touch with the All Mind by reverent gratitude." (Wattles, Wallace. *The Science of Getting Rich*. Holyoke, MA. Elizabeth Towne Company, 1910)

I had never been a tither. While I always considered myself generous with my time and talents, giving money had never been a regular practice for me. The thought of tithing challenged me to think a whole new way. I no longer saw my income as belonging to me. It was a blessing, given to me from God. My job was to be a good steward with what I had, and I wanted to show my gratitude by willingly giving money to God.

Go Toward

When John and his team talked about money, they would talk about what they wanted to give rather than what they wanted to make. It was interesting. They didn't talk about income goals, they talked about giving goals. I loved this thought. I began to realize that I had a skewed perception of money and wealth, that I had been thinking about money in the wrong way. I embraced the concept and decided to begin giving $10 to my church every Sunday.

I know what you're thinking. "Wow, Pam. Aren't you a BIG giver! Ten whole dollars a week!" I know, but remember, I'd never thought about giving like that so I wasn't thinking about giving big. I was thinking about giving consistently and $10 seemed like the right amount at the time. I had a little cushion in my savings account and the promise of a few more paychecks coming in.

Like the verse in Zechariah we spoke about earlier, "Do not despise these small beginnings, for the Lord rejoices to see the work begin..." (NLT). My goal may have been small, but it was a start.

My Shrinking Savings

When I returned from Florida, I faithfully put my $10 in the offering plate every Sunday. I felt joy each week, knowing I was giving back gratefully.

But as the months passed I watched my savings account dwindle. There was no scheduled work on the calendar, no more teacher money coming in and I still had bills to pay. I was becoming more frugal and every week it became a little harder to put money in the plate. But I kept giving.

I'll have to admit; I was getting nervous. I wanted to believe that all would be well, but I was feeling a lot of doubt. I began to scale back on my living expenses. I set my furnace at a chilly 52 degrees, so my heating bill wouldn't be too high. I slept in a sweatshirt and stocking hat to stay warm through the night.

I unplugged everything electrical that I wasn't using because I had read that lights and small appliances continue to pull juice even when they're turned off. I was trying to cut back wherever I could. I looked under the sofa cushions, collected all my loose change in the house and cashed it in at the bank. Cheap food like ramen noodles, mac and cheese and hot dogs became my steady diet. Things were getting tight.

One day, a friend invited me to join her for the Women's Leadership Conference being held in Dubuque. I was intrigued and wanted to attend, but when I looked in my bank account all I had was $36. Reality slapped me hard in the face. I was stung with the realization that I only had $36 to my name. My savings was gone, no business on the books, and nothing coming in. My summer paychecks were gone; my "padding" in savings was gone. $36 was all I had left. $36 total.

I stared at my computer screen and began to cry. For the first time I felt the impact of my decision and realized I was in financial trouble. Tears streaked my cheeks as I thought about the decision I had made to leave my stable teaching job. What had I done? I remembered the comments about this being a mid-life crisis. Were they right? Had I been a fool to think I could totally change careers at this point in my life?

Living the Decision

Thank goodness I have a rock solid inner circle of friends. The kind of friends who speak right to my heart in my darkest hours to remind me of who and Whose I am.

My friend encouraged me and reminded me about Luke 12:7, "Indeed, the very hairs of your head are all numbered. Don't be afraid; you are worth more than many sparrows." (NIV)

He said, "This isn't a mid-life crisis. You're going to be okay. God has counted every hair on your head. He knows you better than anyone else and He will provide everything you need. He provides for the birds, don't you think He'll provide for you? Stay true! When you're going through Hell, don't stop. Keep living the decision you made!"

His faith was a huge lift and, in that instant, I believed he was right. But my reality continued to mess with my mind. I believed that all things are working for my good, but I also knew I only had $36 and Sunday was coming.

I tried to figure out ways to get around my commitment. I began to barter with God, trying to come up with a way out. Maybe I could be sick on Sunday? If I weren't in church, I wouldn't have to give the $10, right? Maybe I could stay home and watch a church service on TV or online? Or maybe I could even go to church but arrive late, after they had already taken up the offering.

I knew how silly the negotiations were, but if there would have been the slightest indication that it would be OK for me to stay home, I certainly would have. But every time I prayed for relief from the obligation to give, there was only silence.

That Sunday I slowly went to church and sat down. I could barely hear the message as I was thinking about the offering coming up. Then, it was time. People all around me began pulling out their purses and billfolds. My heart was pounding. I could see the collection plate going up and down the rows in front of me. Then it was my row. I had my $10 bill concealed in one hand and with the other I accepted the offering basket. I looked toward the ceiling, exhaled and softly whispered to myself, "I believe."

When I had $12,000 in the bank, putting $10 in the plate didn't require much faith. But when all I had was $36, putting $10 in the plate required a whole new level of belief and trust in the Lord.

God Is For Us

Right then, living by faith took on a whole new meaning for me. No one else in church that morning could've known how hard it was for me to put that $10 in the basket. It was such an odd moment. When the basket came by, I dropped in the money and even through my doubts, I felt a tremendous surge of strength. I felt like a poker player with a pair of twos in my hand going all in, pushing all my chips to the middle of the table, believing a winning hand will be in the draw. By that time, my teaching certificate had expired. All my eggs were in my entrepreneurial basket and I thought, *Here we go.*

Today, as I think back, I remember so many hard moments. It was tough to stay true to the belief that God was with me. Every day there was a battle inside, one part wanted to be a strong woman, standing up for what she believed in, pioneering and adventurous. The other part was scared and desperately wanted to go back to the way things were, to direct choirs and live a "secure" life. To return to the comfort that comes with a steady paycheck and knowing what I would be doing every day.

Would I end up selling my house and living with my mom and dad? You can imagine how that scenario played out in my head. I had been a successful high school vocal music director. Through my career, I had built a strong reputation among my colleagues. Now I was faced with the embarrassing possibility of crawling back home in defeat. I had gambled it all on the dream of being an Executive Coach and Team Dynamic

Specialist. Nothing screams "failure" quite like moving back in with your parents when your career crashes. Who would I need to become in order to elevate to this challenge and be successful?

I am not smart enough to fully understand how universal intelligence works, but on that day, it felt as if God had heard me. It was like He knew my situation and, as the kind and loving God that He is, He sent relief. The very next day I got a call from a local company. The facilitator they hired had cancelled on them and they were desperately looking for someone to fill in. "Is there any way you could work with us tomorrow? We can only pay you $500." I had to choke back tears to say, "Of course I can do that!" Thank you, God!

I've learned that even when I think I have a brilliant plan, God may have something else in mind. I've come to a much clearer understanding that my life is not about pushing my agenda on others but rather helping them to discover the unique path that God has for them. And while this is always such an individual quest, we all can use guides along the way to help us discern what could happen through us.

Change the Strategy

I always thought that I would become a giver once I reached a certain level of income. That when I had enough money, I would naturally begin supporting worthy organizations. Guess what? It doesn't work that way. Giving is a mindset as much as it is an action. It doesn't matter if I had $10 or $100,000 to give, the amount wasn't relevant. I wasn't a giver because I wasn't giving.

I was struggling with my thoughts about money and my capacity to make a living. I questioned what I believed about my potential. Was I good enough? Did God really give me the skills and abilities to make it in this new profession? I questioned my ability to make money. Am I a skilled business person? If I give this money away, will there be more money coming in my future? Can I sustain this level of earning? I questioned everything I had ever believed about abundance. Is there really enough for everyone, including me, to have what I want?

Saint Augustine said, "Without God I can't but without me, God won't." So what did I need to learn to be free from this struggle with money?

The answer was simple. *Be Grateful.*

Instead of resisting, enduring, cursing and opposing the situation, change the strategy and simply say, "Thank You." *Thank you* for the opportunity to refine my skills. I don't know what's in my future, but You do, and I trust that all of this is the perfectly preparing me for what's to come. *Thank You.*

When Andrew Carnegie died, a reporter asked his accountant, "How much did he leave behind?" The accountant answered, "All of it." Money, like everything, is simply moving through my life. My responsibility is to be grateful and be a good steward.

Be Grateful! Be Focused! Be Fierce!

Questions:

How would your relationship with struggle change if you believed that all things are working for your good?

What do you believe about what you have?

What do you believe about being a steward of your talent? Your money?

SUMMARY

Life is a beautiful journey filled with a perfect and unique curriculum for each of us. This is our adult playground where we get to become experts at being ourselves and co-creating the life we want to experience. For many people this sounds a little too woo-woo and they disregard it immediately. They would rather fight to remain ineffective, unproductive and joyless. That doesn't seem intelligent to me, but it is an option.

Other people become curious, do the work, embrace accountability for their own life and RISE. They reflect on the significant moments in their life and begin to understand their own map of the world. They see everything as an opportunity to learn, grow and enhance their understanding of the possibility that is moving through their life. They compose their life's masterpiece through actions that align with their desire. They begin using the frequency and unique fingerprint of their voice to add energy, creativity and inspiration to the experience. They feel authentically confident and self-assured knowing that they have the capacity to achieve their goals. They get started knowing that with every step they take, the next step will make itself known. They build healthy relationships because human beings are designed to be connected and express love. They deal with themselves first by examining their thoughts to ensure they are not playing the role of victim in their own life.

And finally, in the last chapter, I used the example of my struggle with giving to teach a lesson of gratitude, but gratitude is not limited to the topic of financial giving. It applies to any struggle in life. As people examine their thoughts and discover their own genius, they change their strategy with struggle.

Here are some thoughts from people who embraced their journey:

"I love how much I learn when I'm doing the heavy lifting and also observing others as they do their lifting. We are all helping each other work toward the common goal of being our best selves with no judgement."

-Jeff Davis, VP Client Experience

"I was surprised how universal the issues are, and the more I apply the lessons, the more in control and at peace I feel."

-Keith Kropp, Assistant VP Product Acquisitions and Strategic Development

"I got tremendous value for all facets of my life. I see a difference in myself and how I deal with my family, my co-workers and people who report to me. My outlook has changed and as a human being I feel 100% better about who I am."

-Danielle Rogers, Accounting Manager

"The switch has not totally flipped, but I'm at a point where I'm aware that I'm not at my best, and I don't like how it feels. Now I know that I don't have to feel this way anymore. The difference between my perception of things and really believing that things are happening for my good has created progress and been a huge step."

-Thomas Sentovich, Associate Acquisitions Manager

Now it's your turn. You get to decide how you'll experience the days that are ahead of you. You get to choose how you're going to show up for yourself, and for the people you love.

I have a picture sitting on my shelf that reads: You are the author of your own life's story. So make it a good one.

Be Focused! Be Fierce! Live a Harmonic Life!

ABOUT

Pamela Mumm, RMT-BC, received her Masters Degree in Music Education at the University of Iowa and her Bachelors Degree with an emphasis on Music Therapy/Music Education/Psychology from Wartburg College. She is a Founding Member of the John Maxwell Training Team and a Floyd Consulting Certified Dream Manager.

Pamela's passion is helping her clients discover and compose a life they love both professionally and personally. In order to achieve her passion, she created the Harmonic Performance® System and Academy: her flagship program focused on helping clients create a happy and unstoppable state of being in order to change the world. She believes that the journey to producing surprising results is best experienced by a team of high functioning individuals working in sync with each other.

When she is not delivering a Keynote Address, leading Strategic Planning Sessions and Workshops, Conducting Executive Coaching Calls or Facilitating Group Coaching Sessions, she can be found on the golf course with her dad, directing the Music Men of Dubuque Barbershop Chorus, or walking her dog.

Website: www.pamelamumm.com

Email: pamela@pamelamumm.com

Thank You

Students of the Wahlert Vocal Music Program from 1995-2011, the parents who supported the Vocal Music students through all those years, Valorie and Kevin Schmitt, Dina Else, Tom Keating, Pamela Hillary, Barry Gentry, Sarah Warthan, Paula Chapin, Paul Martinelli, Dr. William Intriligator, Robert Harrison (Dr. Increase), John Mason, Michael Stairs, Jake Schneider, Chad Chandlee, Doug Warthan, Alec Witters, Bryan VanderLee, Darcy Bailey, the Founding Members of Master Jam, everyone mentioned in the chapters of this book and T.C. Bradley. You have all influenced this book becoming a reality.

Made in the USA
Monee, IL
18 April 2021